DOG EAR

Dog Ear

JIM JOHNSTONE

SIGNAL EDITIONS IS AN IMPRINT OF VÉHICULE PRESS

Published with the generous assistance of The Canada Council for the
Arts and the Canada Book Fund of the Department of Canadian Heritage.

SIGNAL EDITIONS EDITOR: CARMINE STARNINO

Cover design: David Drummond
Photo of author: Patrik Jandak
Set in Filosofia and Minion by Simon Garamond
Printed by Marquis Book Printing Inc.

LIBRARY AND ARCHIVES CANADA CATALOGUING IN PUBLICATION

Johnstone, Jim, 1978-, author
Dog ear / Jim Johnstone.

Poems.
ISBN 978-1-55065-374-8 (pbk.)

1. Title.

PS8619.O489D63 2014   C811'.6   C2014-900595-4

Published by Véhicule Press, Montréal, Québec, Canada
www.vehiculepress.com

Distribution in Canada by LitDistCo
www.litdistco.ca

Distributed in the U.S. by Independent Publishers Group
www.ipgbook.com

Printed in Canada on FSC-certified paper.

C. ndutavo

for Parkdale

- tough guy tone
& de-finishing staging. make
the ordinary strange
yet moments of
tender & ne.

- poetry that resists
linear thinking
or expression
- Anti-lyrical
or perhaps not
overtly lyrical.

Contents

I

Dog Ear 11
Temps Mort 12
First Principles 14
The Fourth Wall 15
Freedom 16
The Greater Good 18

II

Stereophonic 21
Evel Knievel Negotiates the Fountain at Caesar's Palace 22
Casca's Beasts 24
In Defense of Cruelty 25
The Human Projectile 26
Parachute 28

III

Tribeca 31
Louis Dudek, in Love 33
Revenants 34
Sunday Afternoon on the Island of La Grande Jatte 36
Parenthesis 38

IV

The *HMS Hood*, Disarmed 41
Heavy is the Head that Wears the Crown 42
Topiary 43
Against Sense 44
Complementarity 45

V

Inland 49

VI

Post Hoc 59
Love in a Closed System 62
Ariadne's Thread 64
Drive 65
The Approaching Curve 66
Epoch 67

NOTES 70
ACKNOWLEDGEMENTS 71

I

1. what kind of
voice in the
poems? How does it
wish to be understood?
what does it understand?
Is it reliable?

Dog Ear

It was years before I learned to call
this prayer: the right-hand corner
of a page turned down to make another
page. I attempted to escape, then return
to the boneyard where I'd removed
an earring from my wife's right ear—
diamond, the crux of the universe
contracting to leave a pin-sized hole
midair. In that margin, my words
remain transfixed until she disappears—
proof that while I swore the world
I'd created would double like a hand
beneath my own, it merely stretches
before me in consolation. *There, there.*

Temps Mort

Hell is empty. All the devils are here.

    –William Shakespeare, *The Tempest*

Look for a vanishing
point in tooth

and claw, the arrow
that predicts

equal and opposite
circles of hell.

Hell is of this world,
the wind blown

level with rooftops
on New Arthur,

cells re-circulating
as if symmetry

justified existence—
beauty where

nothing beautiful
had been.

Behind my back the
hemisphere

begins again and I
question

whether I'm needed
to complete

this scene: *an open-
ended plain,*

*body dissolving
where a dog-*

*fox circles its tail
until all that*

has passed slows.
When time's

arrow repeats, its bow
empties

and the Devil walks
through.

First Principles

Every time
a swan approaches,
I lean forward
to snap its neck.

Not disposed to
submit,
give ground
where they peck

and peck, the birds
fill the fountain
one by one
like wreck-

ing balls swing-
ing open to
deface
my image. Soon

its clear I'm fucked,
and I turn
to flee
on wingtip shoes—

I never met a man
with one
black eye
who wanted two.

*Passive /
Aggressive
ending.*

The Fourth Wall

Cut to time when time narrows
at the end of a trap-line, the final
generation of a species branching
towards an in-between. Light
in the eye of a hurricane, a chorus
of words that begin in darkness
and end with *know what I mean?*
Mean, for sure, perverse, the shame
of re-buttoning your pants once
you've finished masturbating.
A carnivore at the height
of gluttony, strung out, protean
leash thrashed into a singing chain.

Freedom

Returning to the wall mounted to restrain
its applause, the Assiniboine holds

my reflection as if it holds a sheet of glass:
lips paused, face lined by gables

that tower overhead like a crown.
My first act of free will shall be to believe

in free will penned William James prior
to having his face cast in wax:

the mask—a mantle preserving the strain
of its maker—remains a constant,

hardened thing. The river too has hardened,
each wave refusing the intrusion

of surrounding trees and the juddering
pathway of the bridge; though lit

by more than one source of light,
my presence is hardly sure upon it.

Neither are the red and blue triangles
of canvas moving away like L'Inconnue

de la Seine—free to change direction
with the wind and in the wind change color

with the sky. Looking up, my reflection
remains as my field of vision expands,

having jumped and passed unnoticed
into the flood that threatens the strand.

Local
river
poem.

The Greater Good

Everything I need,
I need now:

the heart's four
walls;

hands expertly
ejecting

pills from the foil
of a blister

pack; valves that
drain

like pigs skewered
on a spit,

spitting fat; control,
or to be loved,

depending on the
greater good.

II

Stereophonic

Underground, current transforms, rounds
into a measured throb of chords. Take
"Train in Vain," broadcast without the sound
of Mick's guitar—all low-end, the quake
of a track revived in a basement
when we were seventeen, lit and flip-
ping though a freight of *Hustlers,* intent
on Johnny Holmes's mustached lip.
We would look, and look again: making
sure we recognized our meager sex
as human, eager for the birth
of Spector's wall after countless takes.
Our hope knew his soundtrack's reflex,
ranged like static in bandwidths of surf.

Evel Knievel Negotiates the Fountain at Caesar's Palace

> Heard myself speak fluently in my own language,
> have heard myself too described as hard work
> (as hard to get through as Scotch broth), though once
> someone rather bladdered told me I was magnetic.
>
> –Roddy Lumsden

Behold my face at a quarter turn: dragonly,
dog-eared, a carnal mask mirroring
half-lit spits of wood. This morning
Nevada furrows, my shoulders
too warm for leather; yet I've no better
armour against the wind, the stagey
palms that threaten to bend and replace
my stationary ramps, Caesar's fountain.
Downrange, I prepare to be bandaged,
hear myself speak fluently in my own language:

"Bridge the strips around my bicep.
It's where I... fuck, not like that. Grip
the razor down-hilt... there. Push...
shit... it won't...". I turn my gaze
towards the melee that surrounds
my bike, making's landfill a network
of forgotten jumps, a backwards glance
before a maelstrom of sand. Derelict,
I've seen how closely my muse lurks,
have heard myself described as hard work:

having the face of an eagle, lion and ox.
Tricked out in off-white chaps, cape,
the valley of the shadow of death,
I gauge the line from rubber to ramp:
uncamp its frame on doubled wings.
Fountain-side, Romans balance,
flock to witness my ramshackle horse couple
with sky: behold my stance,
my corrugated flanks that rake the air, its absence,
(as hard to get through as Scotch broth), though once

I groped around and found myself
unmoored at latitude. What mechanics
hold me, having already landed,
what patience, body tossed ass-first
over the gas-tank's hive? The desert
revives as if in dream: my head a brick,
a helmeted weathervane unraveling
in every plane at once. Lo, it's clear
that this is paradise, and if given a mic
someone rather bladdered will tell me I'm magnetic.

Casca's Beasts

Anime character (handwritten annotation)

The dancers move as if pursued
by Casca's beasts—lions
leaving hesitation marks,
bruises remembered the way
we remember faces
on money, or smoke
that's inhaled but isn't free.
Everyone I've loved
loved me first. The girls,
on their second pass
in search of drinks, flirt,
bend into range when
we throw bills in the air,
make it rain. A shot, a glass
of champagne and lions
prowl the dancefloor.
The DJ keeps time but it takes
more than music to call me
from the women I touch—
money loves me, and those
who love money love me
too. What was it Casca said?
That 'dancer' is a polite
way of saying a girl
hasn't taken off her clothes,
but will, when the right
song plays, and the beasts
set their jaws for the kill.

In Defense of Cruelty

Unnatural,
the shade strung
up behind
a gorilla mask.

I'm not myself
so confess
what you need
to confess:

you're recklessly
content
when set against
my will.

Call me a beast,
a soul
emptied over
an anthill—

I love the way
anger deforms
the bridge
of your snout.

I love the slap
of failure,
what people mean
by down and out.

The Human Projectile

The desire to fly is an idea handed down to us by our ancestors
who, in their grueling travels across trackless lands in prehistoric
times, looked enviously on the birds soaring freely through space,
at full speed, above all obstacles, on the infinite highway of the air.

–Wilbur Wright

What is past, or passing, darkens en route
to the coast, descends like a bird
conjured to distract from a retiring
sleeve, like lampblack, flanks blown
into a cloud of wings. Though burned
I scan the horizon for an incendiary,
the cast of a cannon's neck, the cannon
at rest where earlier I beat its stern
and bragged I'd disappear, a deity
pedaling past the Pacific's crests.

Now, drawn forth in cervical collar
my head aches and a new awareness
pains my senses: single-limbed, bare—
body wed to the stretch of road where
ground reeled out like music and left
its notes upon my brow. Magnetized—
is that the word?—picked first to play
Pompey, I see limbs splayed deaf
as if they aren't my own, hands sized
to fill the bowels of a metal nose

with their ticking. That nose (reclaimed
by Bonaparte) defines a generation's
pleasure: how it drools like a snout!
See its semblance in the earth's curve,
the caress of a lover shunned

by the sun turning from face to face?
Doctor? Doctor, leave me to rule
in these shrived robes, less man
than hill of sand, less sand than wind
deferred to the sky's angled fall and stop.

Parachute

Packed, it rests
its wings
like a vampire
bat, a cape
branded
by scaffolding
that mimics
its spine. At
ten and two
the heavens
open—judge
deferring
to executioner,
shrapnel
reassembled
bearing
the inscription
KEEP CALM
AND CONTINUE
TO SIN. How
close can one
be brought
to the ground
without
touching? Pull
the cord
and suffer
each vertebrae's
dislocation,
the big bang
of a second skin.

III

Tribeca

Bryten Edward Goss, 2006

At dusk, smoke rises
from Tribeca
like an ampersand,

a cirrus cloud
riling sentinels
from the rooftop

where we hover,
Janus-faced
at the sight of flame.

It was Matthew
who warned
that beasts would turn—

and turning, pass
from body
to body until the city

began to burn.
In the conflagration
your dress

swells, peels back
like the mast
of a tall ship—

the marquee dwarfed
by the advancing
proof of motion.

Shifting frames
I submit
to its constraint,

the petal-shaped
hooves
of your composite.

Louis Dudek, in Love

Umbrella held aloft like paper pulled
from a piñata, we trace the limits
of Marie-Reine-du-Monde and bull
inside. Bad luck: the basilica chaste
save for the confetti of our entrance,
the incline of a room within a room
inked-in in happenstance. By chance,
we've stumbled on our Waterloo:
elderly parishioners lulled to sleep,
pews like broken fingers on a working
hand. I take yours now, know your grip,
the clots that bulge like latticework,
confine the prize of blood's ascent.
See here? Your skin grows lean. Exeunt.

descriptive,

Revenants ✓

Jack Chambers, *Lunch*, (1970-)

Snow gathers in the unfinished square
beneath our dining room table,
snow advancing with the New Year,
tracked from yard to yard like light
arrayed in glass. This morning
we're listening for church bells,
it being Sunday, and quiet except
for the branch of an elm scraping
the side of the house where my father
clears a path. It's his unease
that keeps me tethered to my chair,
the expanding drift of his voice
that fills me in a way God never could—
not even as shadow-crosses
darken the edge of the east-facing
window, and snow is reshaped,
piled upon itself to reveal my name
carved into the ground below.
Snow is like a handwritten note,
the muscle memory needed to recreate
each letter on a ledger's grid,
track ink from well to page.
Past noon he enters, his arms flushed
red, raw after laying the front yard
flat enough that Magi could move
across it to gather for a minor king.
In the light, everything beyond the table
sings—the ascent of a knife
withdrawn to stake a claim to reckless-
ness, to complaint, the scar

where a blade locked in my palm
and drew shrieks as I flagged against
the courtyard's frame. I dropped the black
wave of the switchblade's handle
as quickly as it opened, watched
its skeleton bloom like water under
the frozen sheath of a lake. The same blade
is lost now, set where my brother
inscribed the wet curl of my name
in cement. If it had happened otherwise—
father forfeiting his reign over our house,
as blind as Lear to Edgar upon the heath—
would we rise and preside over
this meal in kinship? At the window
a tourniquet of leaves mount
like revenants repeating the radio's
incantations: *we are His flock,*
He doth us feed—the push and pull
of bodies reentering the sky's
middle distance. There
church bells snarl with the clarity
of the father, son, and holy ghost.

Sunday Afternoon on the Island
of La Grande Jatte ✓

Georges Seurat, 1884

Some days, bathers.
Others an endless
stream of bodies
gathered like waves
veiled from the sun
for a century. Still,
the color's not right—
mercury welling
in the vermillion
that spots a dress,
draws a monkey
from the afternoon's
shade. To look
upon this world
is to hold a note
long enough to still
the Seine, hesitate
until I'm one
with the crowd
where you careen
like overlapping
points of light.
At dusk I find you
admiring sails
that emerge in
the east, address you
in the presence
of a cornetist:

Mademoiselle, allow
me to hold
your parasol while
you dab paint
against my lips. Like
this. No, *like this.*

*nice
painting
poem
my fav
so for*

Parenthesis

An umbrella, rungs cuffed,
upturned by the wind.
The bell

of a tuba, quartered,
its embrace when prone.
Tone, swell,

the meridian parting time
and space. A cassette
rewound

centripetally, played
back at the speed
of sound.

The tight-lipped mouth
of a renowned
ventriloquist.

IV

The *HMS Hood*, Disarmed

WAR poem.

For three minutes the *Hood*
shouldered the paunch
of salt and flame flooding

its pores, clutched
a cyclone to its Saturday
finest. Bulkheads closed,

fifth salvo of shells an act
of kindness, only the fog
felt the ocean pull

quicker. It was the year
the Alaska highway
unfurled its tongue, long

before a piano tumbled
through the Aquitania's ballroom
ceiling—the seascape complete

with a chandelier of keys,
a drowned wheel
and three new ways to cross the ocean.

Heavy is the Head that Wears the Crown

The ocean's shield
foreclosing, you called
from a payphone
that hissed when you spoke:

Gone are the days
in Sackville Park,
Turing's statue
replaced with goodwill.

I walked up, bowed,
and bit into his apple—
spat at onlookers
while I chewed aloud.

Remember the cipher
we misread, holding
its message between us
like barbed wire?

We thought ourselves
kings, the fire
necessary to extinguish
code that said:

It's impossible to wear
the crown
without the bullet that follows
entering the head.

Topiary

Between hedgerows your mind's
fox slows its feet, stills the thistled
fleece it tows behind.

Fleece or flag unwound—
a warning draped to fall
between hedgerows: *mind*

the quarry assigned
a human role, the charcoal
towed behind

a discharged rifle. Its sudden
bolt incises a mantle
between hedgerows, your mind

composed, a clearing blind
to the rabble
of passersby towed behind

in shadow. They linger downwind
as you steal
between hedgerows, your mind
a fleece you tow behind.

Against Sense

Bonjour tristesse: up all night fidgeting
with your corsage, luggage roped
to a kite. When in Rome, gullage begets
gullage, fingers trained to scope
fatigues, rustle up a handsome sum.
Still, you linger: fox-headed, faunal,
driven underground with the soon
to be hunted hawk, black-faced cardinal.
All this and I've forgotten the Fawkes
of penny dreadfuls, last seen in silver,
augered to a ring. Lets lift our rocks
O Blue Bloods, and pitch from cover
into his parade: bodily, tusk-sleeved,
against sense. *Adieu tristesse*, take your leave.

Complementarity

I frisk your lips with a mouthful
of brass, insist on bluster
just to be sure. Sure enough,
the trombone speaks—fills
the hanger with its signature,
the echo needed to map
your descent, seconds earlier.
All that's lost is given shape—
a hand crushed under *Boeing*
fuselage, the burgeoning
chevrons strewn across your
brow. My own hands reposition,
work to create the notes
you knew as if they were
a well-loved prosthesis.
Takemitsu's soundtrack to
The Face of Another, or a song
just like it. Brother, I could
reconstruct your armature,
lead you back to the scaffolding
and never guess your curse.
Ignore the medics, death's
momentum and its intermittent
compliments. Find your peace.

V

Inland

1.

Left unaided to temper the seam of
a mechanical wing, we release our
cloak-pins, set to kindling flares. Above,
jays alight where earlier we scoured
the heavens for cover, the heavens gone
dark over solitary tracks. Exiled,
grounded in bile, piss; our maps redrawn
on survey; we limp from the audible
hiss of the river, fuselage flooding
with surf. Here remnants console, stir
our hunger for beauty: razed shells, studs,
rosin spilled on contact with an arbor
of pine. Negotiating distance, flames
diverge, forsake the sky for coming rain.

forest-fire rescue.

2.

Flames diverge, forsake the sky; a bitter
plinth of sun. It seems an age we spurned
the earth, its bow and quake, tow interred
in the ocean's relief. '41; terns
rose from Bonavista Bay, clipped Banting
in escort to the Old World. Light work
his drop, his desperation. Winter's slant
right angled into passage; the same fork
that drew our *Beaver* to mire, united
wheel and weight. Newly transient, old growth
afire, we cling to suitcases like
folding armor; Ulysses' kin rowing
our breastplates to shore. Instrument, hostile
lover, we follow the river for miles.

3.

Love, we follow the river for miles:
cut nascent tracks, pace its glacial shell.
A day, two perhaps, and fever riles
our guts, sets my compass to a hell
renewed by famine. Fireweed, black spruce,
balsam: frozen talismans, paperweights
we plunder for a means to heal. No use
tunneling, worrying winter's seal; hate
gives way to panic, metal to bark; form
deformed with each inexpert blow.
I gasp, newly pneumonic, a storm
of alveolar blood spewed-up in snow:
clots softened, excess a lithograph we
inhabit with a leper's mastery.

4.

Smoke a lithograph, a leper's signal
we've learned to distrust. Miles back, rain
spoiled our carrion; its diurnal
warning dispersed like a peacock drained
of color. And what of winter's soot,
our haven's upturned roots? Before us,
the Appalachians lift above the foot-
hills, mute our shovels; our ex-pilot
bared of his rifle and interred in a
makeshift shroud. Ornament, his gun, without
ammunition; trigger an apical
tick, comfort surrendered to frostbite, gout.
When coyotes near our camp we depart,
their cries revelatory, claws alert.

5.

Our cries are revelatory, hopeful
at the first hint of an enclosure.
Closer, an orphaned cow emerges; dull
eyes fenced in a sash of fur, burrs
obscuring recognition. A sure thing,
domesticity, the span of rail
assembled to betray our wandering.
Network of decay, ancestry, veil.
Sea-light despite the ocean's darkening
cloak, our estuary's muddy tongue.
Overhead, revelation's ruddy mark
extends like venom, an unnoticed hue:
silver, the flame kindled to ablate
an abandoned foundation, tout suite.

6.

An abandoned foundation: barrow,
manure, fiberglass; furnace oil
echoing my hand at flint: now, now,
now and the otherness of fire, soil
soldered to the cabin's melted ground-
work. Unbridled, we set our mark upon
this domicile like mutts; dogs wounding
dogs until Penelope's arrow yawns
and collapses in a rut. God's tinder-
box an unsteady muse, a lapse in prayer:
for thine is the kingdom, the disorder
in my breast for ever and ever.
Saved, anchored to our disgrace, we bend
to tame the river's flux. Somnambulant.

7.

Grace. A helicopter tames the river's
flux, lumbers over a flock of trailing
geese. At last we forgo deliverance,
nature's trespass; the crux of our failure
a few sticks of wood, the plateau of green
where we regenerate, birdlike.
Everywhere at once, the weather's mean:
flatlands furrowed, windows spiked
with hail; marram resistant as we bi-
sect the horizon. Monastic blades
fashion a cross over the sun. Scythe
hearted, our company's shade
lifts likeness from stands of birch, blots
retreating lanes of wind: our pilot.

8.

Effaced by retreat, lanes of wind fix
our flag to Pearson's tarmac: one and one
and one seeding backfields with brick
and bone. In abeyance, bridges have gone
slack; my return clubfooted, barbed
with disease. *Fee-fi-fo-fum, I crop my
beard like an Englishman*. Scissored, I cede
to instinct: finally barefoot, propped
against a bathroom mirror. Charged to strip
the dirt from my reflection I leave
the worry to my double, drift
towards a single mattress, the quiet cave
of your arms. Pieced together like worms,
we resist exchange. The sun tempers our seams.

VI

Post Hoc

It was a hunch that drove me there,
Bishamon, harried by fortune
on the loveliest day of the year.
Daffodils at the eaves,

cattails drenched in a hand-watered
square. Back home the hunt
had begun, my covenant
with muscle and bone

bartered for thirst—an oak table
where one of the help
had whittled a tern
to drown in its only able sea.

The miracle of birth filled me.
Johnny Black and fistic
revelries over the usual—
a woman, fate,

the blacksmith's missing thumb.
I'd always known it gone,
supplanted by a grip
sound enough to shoe a cloven

hoof. *The Devil* they'd say,
but I'd seen worse—
men who'd tired of shooting
bottles and aimed

in my direction. Who was I
if not prophet? Come to settle
that the 'smith threw first—
a rabbit-punch,

sure in line with the barkeep's jaw.
Dorsal spurred, I thrust
my weight upon
the nearest prow in grief,

caught a rabid blow for my worry.
The 'smith kept silent
at the till, watched daylight
vex a slur of blood.

It was luck security ran me out.
I fled in time
with neighboring beagles,
flushed rabbits from a flood

of brush. Or at least mimed pursuit
until I found a clearing
for the dogs to go about
their work. Rugged stuff that,

warrens fogged with vox angelica,
battered teeth.
Even clouds stopped
to admire the choir of jaws—

their ragged hallelujah of grief.
Bending forth to join,
I stole away my share
of marrow, thawed fingers

in a shroud of dirt. Only then did I
understand the need
to inter my bounty,
spread its ribs before my feet.

Love in a Closed System

$$m_1 u_1 + m_2 u_2 = (m_1 + m_2)\, v$$

Love: it's what I've always
known—arm thrust

toward an inexhaustible point
on the horizon

like a flare, temporal and set.
Wherever. Where

we met. This thoroughfare our
lone destination,

bodies soaring above two feet
of snow,

linked by a leather wheel.
I remember

the calm—dirt shoulder hedged
with rime,

refuse, a parade of egrets pacing
the woods.

I remember the bewildered
wedge of hoods,

steel forced into a kiss. Connect
and disconnect—

your arm a twisted leaf, muscle
doubled back

and helpless beneath my own.
My hand forces

an exit, movement where earlier
we had progressed

with fused elegance, unspeaking.
Unspeaking still,

I bow where snow begins to fix
its frozen quills.

'fused elegance'
is a good
description of
your poems

Ariadne's Thread

At ten feet, the white oak's boughs begin
their reach, parse Niagara's brow
with lines of Morse: *long dash, long dash,*
sky—our limbs twinned with snow
at each iamb's incline. Deigned to set,
confound shadow like a nascent thrush,
light sweeps into the wind's rough socket.
Our pact: to climb against winter's rush—
mad, uncoupled—fighting the advance
of latent incantations. Such is our mutiny,
less smirk than shitface grin, less stance
than having failed to plant our feet.
Rewind and we descend like ticks wrenched
from blood, from alveolar branches.

a harsh, strange kind of love-making.

Drive

No one will find us in this city—not your valentine,
not the line of dogs he's chained by the throat. My collar
blooms chin-high, is perfumed with lilac where you
finger buttons, parse leaves and hook a flush of green

to my breast. Tell me you're good. Tell me we'll
lend our touch to the nearest MG, drive south on a
sucker bet until we run dry in the desert. There are
others who've come uninvited, who've come to free

themselves from their skin, lose their grip
and trace in a mess of coins. Here's my loss—fist
lodged in the maw of the first guest to speak, our
honour run aground. To stay we'll need to slap down

the pin that adorns your jacket, bet against a snail being
able to survive the edge of a straight razor. I've been
told that nothing can live to know such a lean blade.
When we drive land rises and we rise with it.

tough guy
or his moll

The Approaching Curve

You said we could be happy
anywhere. But here?
Scylla's cavern haunts our map.
You said we could be happy
unlipped, unvoiced; left to clap
along or disappear.
You said we could be happy
anywhere but here.

Epoch

$$f^*, C(f^*) \leq C(f) \; f \; F$$

Forming and reforming the sun seems
to urge Edward VII into motion—
arms slack, horse reared to match
the parabola of its hooves. Lit by proxy,
I place my index finger in line with
a bronze leg, hold still enough to see
clouds break into smaller clouds, shroud
Cerberus patrolling the Queen's gates.
Let us descend into the blind world—
or at least a muted reproduction where
I dig a penknife into the horse's hide
as sure as if Degas had gouged the line
himself. I'm not the first to autograph
this monument—earlier its scrotum
was painted gold, a second sun rising
as weight decreased counter to its spine.
When protracted, this measurement
is a match for the mural that backs
our loft: vermillion, veined with sulfur,
paint affixed like blood that's lingered
too long in an inverted head. Before
tidewater calved and bore spring's leftover
advance, its fresco of fallen branches,
it was a neighborhood girl who fell
the length of brick and paint to land
below our second-story window.
I was there when she took to sky, dove
with arms outstretched from the middle
of the sun. Later, we learned her flight
a push, were witness to the vandal who

arrived to append wings to the remains
of her outline, chalk feathered where her
fingers spread twenty-six floors, an angel's
pallium, jeans hugging her thighs like
a second skin. Skin a parchment forming
and reforming, gold, the color you'd paint
your face before we'd move backwards
through our days, settle into lives
unmenaced by the grin cut into the dead
girl's mouth. Morning glory then, lamps
lit to clarify shapes that came before—
each lover a knot, a synapse doubled
back and trapped inside the brainpan's
conch. You're one among a collection
of shells in the park where we light joints
and toss them, filterless, into Edward
VII's crotch, paint peeling back like waves
returning to the Holocene. Teeming with
the thrill of a wound we cheer, reverie's
fog possessed of an audible hunger
as crows wheel overhead. Like a sheet
we've loitered beneath with notions of rest
the sky is suddenly dark, sulfur lamps
diffuse before steel can stoop to illuminate
new men crafting new manners of love.

NOTES

'Temps Mort' incorporates a line from Antonin Artaud's *General Security: The Liquidation of Opium*.

'First Principles' incorporates lines from Paul Muldoon's *Quoof*.

The epigraph to 'Evel Knievel Negotiates the Fountain at Caesar's Palace' is taken from the poem 'Self Portrait as Hard Work' in Roddy Lumsden's *Third Wish Wasted*.

'In Defense of Cruelty' incorporates lyrics from the Led Zeppelin song 'Black Dog.'

In 'Sunday Afternoon on the Island of La Grande Jatte,' the line "Some days, bathers" is adapted from the line "Some days, jugglers" in Stephanie Bolster's *A Page from the Wonders of Life on Earth*.

The epigraph to 'Against Sense' is taken from Paul Eluard's 'À Peine Défigurée.'

'Epoch' incorporates lines from Dante's *Inferno*, as translated by A. S. Kline.

Acknowledgments

Some of the poems in *Dog Ear* have previously appeared in *Arc Poetry Magazine, Canadian Notes & Queries, Contemporary Verse 2, en Route, The Fiddlehead, Maisonneuve, Matrix, The Moth (UK), The New Quarterly, Prism International, Riddle Fence, Taddle Creek, This Magazine, Vallum, The Walrus* and the limited edition chapbook *Epoch* (Frog Hollow Press, 2013).

'Against Sense' was performed on CBC Radio 1's *Here and Now*.

'Dog Ear' was nominated for the 2014 Pushcart Prize.

'Epoch' won *Matrix Magazine*'s 2011 LitPop Award for Poetry.

'Evel Knievel Negotiates the Fountain at Caesar's Palace' took first prize in the poetry category of *This Magazine*'s 2010 Great Canadian Literary Hunt. It was also anthologized in *A Crystal Through Which Love Passes: Glosas for P.K. Page* (Buschek Books, 2013).

'Inland' was anthologized in *Best Canadian Poetry in English 2012* (Tightrope Books).

'Louis Dudek, in Love' was published as a broadside by Frog Hollow Press.

'Parenthesis' was published as a broadside by the Toronto Poetry Vendors.

'Revenants' was an Editor's Choice in *Arc Poetry Magazine*'s 2013 Poem of the Year Contest, and was anthologized in *Play: An Anthology of Poems About Children* (Frog Hollow Press, 2014).

'Sunday Afternoon on the Island of La Grande Jatte' won *The Fiddlehead*'s 2012 Ralph Gustafson Poetry Prize, and was published as a broadside by Baseline Press.

A previous version of this book was shortlisted for the 2012 K.M. Hunter Artist Award in Literature.

My thanks to both the Ontario Arts Council and the Toronto Arts Council for funding that aided me in the composition of this book.

Signal
EDITIONS

Carmine Starnino, Editor
Michael Harris, Founding Editor

SELECTED POEMS David Solway
THE MULBERRY MEN David Solway
A SLOW LIGHT Ross Leckie
NIGHT LETTERS Bill Furey
COMPLICITY Susan Glickman
A NUN'S DIARY Ann Diamond
CAVALIER IN A ROUNDHEAD SCHOOL Errol MacDonald
VEILED COUNTRIES/LIVES Marie-Claire Blais (Translated by Michael Harris)
BLIND PAINTING Robert Melançon (Translated by Philip Stratford)
SMALL HORSES & INTIMATE BEASTS Michel Garneau
    (Translated by Robert McGee)
IN TRANSIT Michael Harris
THE FABULOUS DISGUISE OF OURSELVES Jan Conn
ASHBOURN John Reibetanz
THE POWER TO MOVE Susan Glickman
MAGELLAN'S CLOUDS Robert Allen
MODERN MARRIAGE David Solway
K. IN LOVE Don Coles
THE INVISIBLE MOON Carla Hartsfield
ALONG THE ROAD FROM EDEN George Ellenbogen
DUNINO Stephen Scobie
KINETIC MUSTACHE Arthur Clark
RUE SAINTE FAMILLE Charlotte Hussey
HENRY MOORE'S SHEEP Susan Glickman
SOUTH OF THE TUDO BEM CAFÉ Jan Conn
THE INVENTION OF HONEY Ricardo Sternberg
EVENINGS AT LOOSE ENDS Gérald Godin (Translated by Judith Cowan)
THE PROVING GROUNDS Rhea Tregebov
LITTLE BIRD Don Coles
HOMETOWN Laura Lush
FORTRESS OF CHAIRS Elisabeth Harvor
NEW & SELECTED POEMS Michael Harris
BEDROCK David Solway
TERRORIST LETTERS Ann Diamond
THE SIGNAL ANTHOLOGY Edited by Michael Harris
MURMUR OF THE STARS: SELECTED SHORTER POEMS Peter Dale Scott
WHAT DANTE DID WITH LOSS Jan Conn
MORNING WATCH John Reibetanz
JOY IS NOT MY PROFESSION Muhammad al-Maghut
    (Translated by John Asfour and Alison Burch)
WRESTLING WITH ANGELS: SELECTED POEMS Doug Beardsley
HIDE & SEEK Susan Glickman
MAPPING THE CHAOS Rhea Tregebov
FIRE NEVER SLEEPS Carla Hartsfield
THE RHINO GATE POEMS George Ellenbogen
SHADOW CABINET Richard Sanger
MAP OF DREAMS Ricardo Sternberg
THE NEW WORLD Carmine Starnino
THE LONG COLD GREEN EVENINGS OF SPRING Elisabeth Harvor
KEEP IT ALL Yves Boisvert (Translated by Judith Cowan)
THE GREEN ALEMBIC Louise Fabiani

THE ISLAND IN WINTER Terence Young
A TINKERS' PICNIC Peter Richardson
SARACEN ISLAND: THE POEMS OF ANDREAS KARAVIS David Solway
BEAUTIES ON MAD RIVER: SELECTED AND NEW POEMS Jan Conn
WIND AND ROOT Brent MacLaine
HISTORIES Andrew Steinmetz
ARABY Eric Ormsby
WORDS THAT WALK IN THE NIGHT Pierre Morency
    (Translated by Lissa Cowan and René Brisebois)
A PICNIC ON ICE: SELECTED POEMS Matthew Sweeney
HELIX: NEW AND SELECTED POEMS John Steffler
HERESIES: THE COMPLETE POEMS OF ANNE WILKINSON, 1924-1961
    Edited by Dean Irvine
CALLING HOME Richard Sanger
FIELDER'S CHOICE Elise Partridge
MERRYBEGOT Mary Dalton
MOUNTAIN TEA Peter Van Toorn
AN ABC OF BELLY WORK Peter Richardson
RUNNING IN PROSPECT CEMETERY Susan Glickman
MIRABEL Pierre Nepveu (Translated by Judith Cowan)
POSTSCRIPT Geoffrey Cook
STANDING WAVE Robert Allen
THERE, THERE Patrick Warner
HOW WE ALL SWIFTLY: THE FIRST SIX BOOKS Don Coles
THE NEW CANON: AN ANTHOLOGY OF CANADIAN POETRY
    Edited by Carmine Starnino
OUT TO DRY IN CAPE BRETON Anita Lahey
RED LEDGER Mary Dalton
REACHING FOR CLEAR David Solway
OX Christopher Patton
THE MECHANICAL BIRD Asa Boxer
SYMPATHY FOR THE COURIERS Peter Richardson
MORNING GOTHIC: NEW AND SELECTED POEMS George Ellenbogen
36 CORNELIAN AVENUE Christopher Wiseman
THE EMPIRE'S MISSING LINKS Walid Bitar
PENNY DREADFUL Shannon Stewart
THE STREAM EXPOSED WITH ALL ITS STONES D.G. Jones
PURE PRODUCT Jason Guriel
ANIMALS OF MY OWN KIND Harry Thurston
BOXING THE COMPASS Richard Greene
CIRCUS Michael Harris
THE CROW'S VOW Susan Briscoe
WHERE WE MIGHT HAVE BEEN Don Coles
MERIDIAN LINE Paul Bélanger (Translated by Judith Cowan)
SKULLDUGGERY Asa Boxer
SPINNING SIDE KICK Anita Lahey
THE ID KID Linda Besner
GIFT HORSE Mark Callanan
SUMPTUARY LAWS Nyla Matuk
THE GOLDEN BOOK OF BOVINITIES Robert Moore
MAJOR VERBS Pierre Nepveu (Translated by Donald Winkler)
ALL SOULS' Rhea Tregebov
THE SMOOTH YARROW Susan Glickman
THE GREY TOTE Deena Kara Shaffer
HOOKING Mary Dalton
DANTE'S HOUSE Richard Greene
BIRDS FLOCK FISH SCHOOL Edward Carson
SATISFYING CLICKING SOUND Jason Guriel
DOG EAR Jim Johnstone

- music
- painting

make ordinary not strange. Mornings.

Like the "page turned down to make another / page," *Dog Ear* explores the marks we leave on a world whose social and political markers are constantly shifting. In his fourth book of poems—and most powerful work to date—Jim Johnstone establishes himself as an exquisite observer of decay, both physical and spiritual. This is a universe where man resembles "the final / generation of a species branching / towards an in-between." Johnstone's poetry blurs past and present, private and public in a kinetic style marked by weird semi-narratives, defamiliarizing close-ups and raw self-examinations.

Praise for Jim Johnstone:

"There is a lot to admire in *Patternicity*: musicality, intelligence, toughness, tensile juxtapositions of rational enquiry and lyrical tenderness."
– *Arc Poetry Magazine*

"Johnstone's poems are entertaining, erotic, and dangerous, and at times brute in their clean, heart-wrenching details."
– *Mansfield Review*

"Johnstone simply does not miss opportunities to drive home his music, to exploit each vowel's potential to ring and electrify its neighbours."
– *Maple Tree Literary Supplement*

JIM JOHNSTONE is the author of *The Velocity of Escape* (Guernica Editions, 2008), *Patternicity* (Nightwood Editions, 2010) and *Sunday, the locusts* (Tightrope Books, 2011). He is the recipient of a CBC Literary Award, *The Fiddlehead's* Ralph Gustafson Poetry Prize, and *Matrix Magazine's* LitPop Award. Currently he's the poetry editor at Palimpsest Press, and an associate editor at Representative Poetry Online. He lives in Toronto.

$16.00

Cover designed by David Drummond